MARTIAL ARTS
SPORTS ZONE

TAE KWON DO

KOREAN FOOT AND FIST COMBAT

Garrison Wells

Lerner Publications Company • Minneapolis

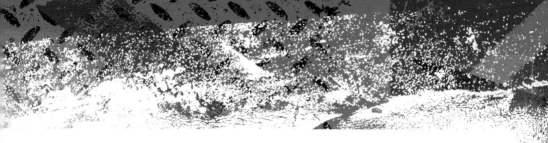

Lerner Publications Company
A division of Lerner Publishing Group, Inc.
241 First Avenue North
Minneapolis, MN 55401 U.S.A.

Website address: www.lernerbooks.com

Content Consultant: Jan Rubsam, third-degree black belt in tae kwon do

Library of Congress Cataloging-in-Publication Data
Wells, Garrison.
    Tae kwon do : Korean foot and fist combat / by Garrison Wells.
        p.   cm. — (Martial arts sports zone)
    Includes index.
    ISBN 978-0-7613-8458-8 (lib. bdg. : alk. paper)
    1. Tae kwon do—Juvenile literature. I. Title.
GV1114.9.W45 2012
796.815'3—dc23   2011037852

Manufactured in the United States of America
1 – BC – 12/31/11

Photo Credits: Adam Pretty/Getty Images, 5; Dreamstime, 6; Matt Dunham/AP Images, 7; Michael Rougier/Time & Life Pictures/Getty Images, 9; Co Rentmeester/Time & Life Pictures/Getty Images, 10; Gerville Hall/iStockphoto, 11, 16, 28; David Appleby/Walt Disney Pictures/Photofest, 12; Paramount Pictures/Photofest, 13; Veronika Surovtseva/Shutterstock Images, 15 (top); Dariusz Kuzminski/Shutterstock Images, 15 (bottom); Eugene Hoshiko/AP images, 17; Fred Dufour/AFP/Getty Images, 18; Kirk Strickland/iStockphoto, 19; Jim West/Alamy, 20; Chung Sung-Jun/Getty Images, 21; Boris Pamikov/Shutterstock Images, 22; Janis Litavnieks/iStockphoto, 23; Rob Wilson/Shutterstock Images, 25; Josh Hedges/Zuffa LLC/Getty Images, 26; Specialpictures.nl/Alamy, 29 (top); Aaron Favila/AP Images, 29 (bottom).
Backgrounds: Aleksandar Velasevic/iStockphoto, Patrick Wong/iStockphoto
Cover: © Jana Leon/Photonica/Getty Images (main); © iStockphoto.com/Aleksandar Velasevic (background).
Main body text set in ITC Serif Gothic Std Bold 11/17.
Typeface provided by Adobe Systems.

TABLE OF CONTENTS

CHAPTER ONE

OVERVIEW OF TAE KWON DO

The 2000 Olympic Games showed off tae kwon do as an official part of the event for the first time. This exciting martial art comes from Korea. It is filled with high-flying kicks and powerful strikes. U.S. athlete Steven Lopez went to the Games in Sydney, Australia, ready to win.

Lopez started learning tae kwon do at the age of five. He worked hard at his sport. He also did well in school. At the Games, his hard work and talent led him to the gold medal in the lightweight division.

THE LOPEZES

Steven won gold again at the 2004 Games. But the 2008 Olympic Games were special for the entire Lopez family. Steven's sister Diana and brother Mark were also part of the U.S. tae kwon do team. Steven and Diana each won a bronze medal. Mark won a silver medal.

Steven Lopez (left) won the gold medal at the 2000 Olympic Games. At the Olympic level, athletes wear protective gear.

For many people, the 2000 Games were their first look at this martial art. Lopez got his victory and helped show tae kwon do to the world.

WHAT IS TAE KWON DO?

Tae kwon do means the "way of the hand and foot" in Korean. This martial art includes punching, kicking, jumping, and blocking. It is a blend of karate, which came from Japan, and *taekkyon*, an ancient Korean fighting style.

A tae kwon do student performs a side piercing kick.

"HAVE BELIEF IN YOURSELF, MAKE THE MOST OF COMPETING AS IT IS OVER BEFORE YOU KNOW IT. NOTHING IS IMPOSSIBLE IF YOU WANT IT BADLY ENOUGH."
—JULIA CROSS, SIX-TIME INTERNATIONAL TAE KWON DO WORLD CHAMPION

Training also includes *kyukpa,* or "breaking power." Skilled athletes are able to break wood and bricks using their bare hands and feet. Sparring (practice fighting) and forms (patterns of moves) are also key parts of training. Some of tae kwon do's stars are Scotland's Julia Cross and U.S. fighters Chuck Norris and Mike Warren.

WHY STUDY TAE KWON DO?

Tae kwon do is widely respected as a good form of self-defense. It is also a challenging sport. Students who are serious about tae kwon do find it physically and mentally demanding. It is also emotionally satisfying. For many people across the globe, studying and mastering tae kwon do is a way of life.

Diana Lopez (left) defeated Italy's Veronica Calabrese (right) in the 2008 Olympic Games to win the bronze medal.

CHAPTER TWO
HISTORY AND CULTURE

In 1930 12-year-old Choi Hong Hi started studying martial arts. He began training in taekkyon in southern Korea. He later studied karate in Japan. He eventually combined the two styles to create his own martial art. It would later become known as tae kwon do.

By 1950 Korea had been divided politically into northern and southern halves. From 1950 to 1953, the two parts were at war against each other. U.S. soldiers fought alongside South Korean troops in the Korean War.

During the war, martial arts masters gathered in South Korea. They showed off their skills and styles in front of South Korean president Syngman Rhee. By this time, Choi was a general in the South Korean army. The martial arts show impressed President Rhee. He knew General Choi was a martial arts master. President Rhee ordered the general to make sure that all South Korean soldiers got martial arts training. Choi also taught U.S. soldiers who were serving in the military.

South Korean president Syngman Rhee (*right*) insisted that all South Korean soldiers be taught tae kwon do.

By 1957 the new martial art style was dubbed tae kwon do. It had become the national sport of South Korea.

SPREAD AROUND THE WORLD

U.S. soldiers brought tae kwon do home with them after the war. Korean masters of the martial art who visited the United States also introduced the sport. Nam Tae Hi, for example, visited the U.S. Army base at Fort Benning, Georgia. He showed people tae kwon do moves while he was there.

SKILLED ATHLETES TAUGHT TAE KWON DO TO THE TIGER DIVISION, SOUTH KOREA'S COMBAT FORCE. THE TIGER DIVISION BECAME A FAMOUS AND HIGHLY TRAINED UNIT.

Members of the Tiger Division train in tae kwon do in 1966.

In the early 1960s, a few masters were called the "original masters of taekwondo." The Korean Taekwondo Association (KTA) ordered these masters to spread the martial art around the world.

ORGANIZING THE MARTIAL ART

One of the largest martial arts organizations in North America is the American Taekwondo Association (ATA). It began when U.S. serviceman Richard Reed returned to the United States from Korea. He invited his Korean tae kwon do teacher, Haeng Ung Lee, to join him.

The two opened a school in Omaha, Nebraska. Together they founded the ATA in 1969. The organization has helped spread tae kwon do across the country.

A tae kwon do student practices a front snap kick, one of the sport's most popular moves.

Jackie Chan (left) has trained in several martial arts, including tae kwon do.

CELEBRITIES WHO PRACTICE

SEVERAL CELEBRITIES STUDY TAE KWON DO. AMONG THEM ARE FORMER PRESIDENT BILL CLINTON AND PROFESSIONAL GOLFER PHIL MICKELSON. ACTOR JACKIE CHAN HAS ALSO STUDIED TAE KWON DO. IN 2011 HE WON A KIDS' CHOICE AWARD FOR FAVORITE BUTTKICKER IN THE REMAKE OF THE KARATE KID.

The ATA has ties to the Songahm Taekwondo Federation (STF). Seven countries in South America belong to the STF. The ATA is also connected to the World Traditional Taekwondo Union (WTTU). This organization runs tournaments in Canada, Britain, and Portugal. It also holds events in Germany, South Africa, Japan, and Sweden.

IMPACT ON CULTURE

As tae kwon do spread, it began to influence culture outside martial arts. Tae kwon do has found its way into movies and computer games and onto TV. The film *Tekken* (2010) features tae kwon do. It is based on the video game of the same name, which came out in the mid-1990s.

In 2008 *The Rebel* was released in the United States. It starred Vietnamese martial artist and stuntman Johnny Tri Nguyen. He used his tae kwon do skills in the movie. He also used them as a stuntman in *Spider-Man* and *Spider-Man 2*. In 2010 tae kwon do star Noah Ringer starred as Aang in *The Last Airbender*.

In the computer games arena, the fighting game *Taekwon-Do* has become popular. It first came out in 1994. In the game, players fight in a tae kwon do tournament using actual attacks and tournament rules. In 2010 the similar game *Taekwon-Do World Champion* was released.

Noah Ringer used his tae kwon do skills in *The Last Airbender*.

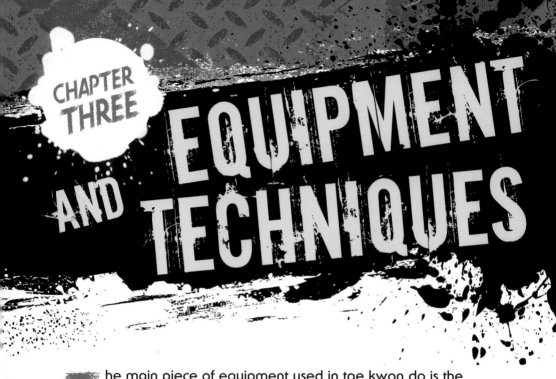

CHAPTER THREE

EQUIPMENT AND TECHNIQUES

The main piece of equipment used in tae kwon do is the *dobok*, or uniform. It consists of white pants and a white top. The top is closed at the front in a *V* shape. A belt is tied around the waist. The belt shows the student's skill level. Beginning students start with a white belt. They move up to black belt. This is the highest belt color in tae kwon do. However, many organizations have several degrees of black belt.

BELTS

In tae kwon do, belts have a meaning beyond rank. Each color shows growth. The white belt stands for purity. Yellow and orange belts are the color of the rising sun, helping seeds begin to grow. Green is the next belt, showing the seeds sprouting and growing. Blue and purple stand for the color of the sky. Students try to reach these levels as they move up in rank. Brown stands for the ground. At this level, students have a solid foundation of skills. Red is the color of blood, necessary for all life. Black, the highest belt level, is all colors together.

A tae kwon do student wears his dobok during training. The green belt shows he has reached the fourth level of tae kwon do.

Students wear protective gear to make sparring safer.

Tae kwon do students also use safety gear for sparring. Students spar so they can practice punching, kicking, and blocking. The moves are not practiced at full power. But students still often wear safety gear. This may include a chest protector, gloves, forearm guards, and shin guards. A groin cup, headgear, and a mouth guard are also worn. Different organizations and clubs call for different safety gear during competitions.

During a side piercing kick, the leg can be raised very high into the air.

Tae kwon do is practiced in a *dojang*, or gym. Schools usually have hardwood floors or mats and mirrors on the wall. They also have equipment to practice striking and punching. Large heavy bags for striking often hang from the ceiling.

TECHNIQUES

Kicking is important in tae kwon do because of the power and reach of the legs. Some of the world's most beautiful and complicated kicks come from tae kwon do.

The most common kicks include the front snap kick, the side piercing kick, the axe kick, and the roundhouse kick. Some kicks have both jumping and spinning. Those include the jumping spinning roundhouse kick and the butterfly kick.

Jumping and spinning can be added to just about any kick. There's a difference between a jumping kick and a flying kick. In the jumping kick, a person jumps straight up before kicking. In the flying kick, a person actually runs and then jumps before the kick.

In an axe kick, a competitor brings the leg down onto an opponent's head.

Using blocks successfully (*left*) is a necessary part of sparring.

PUNCHES

Tae kwon do isn't just about kicking, however. It is a balanced martial art that also includes punches and strikes. Fighters aim punches and strikes at specific targets. These are mostly the face and the torso. A hammer fist uses the outside of the fist to strike the face. The back fist uses the back of the fist as the striking surface. The knife hand is an open hand strike. It uses the outside edge of the hand. Tae kwon do also uses elbow strikes in board breaking and self-defense.

BLOCKS

Fighters use blocks in tae kwon do to avoid an attacker. Each block is used to stop a specific attack. The single forearm block is used against kicks at the body. The low block is used to defend low attacks to both the body and the legs. The rising block defends attacks to the head.

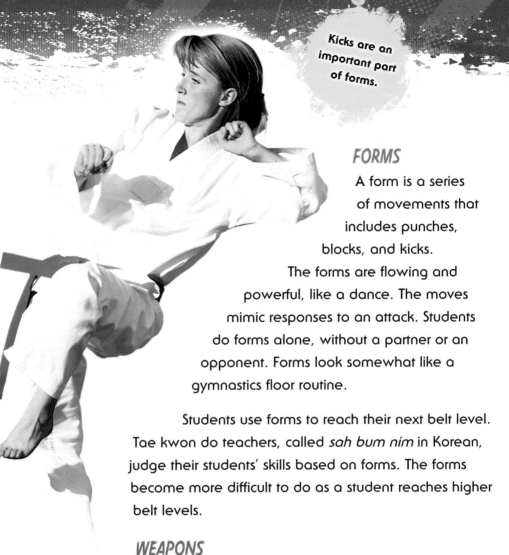

Kicks are an important part of forms.

FORMS

A form is a series of movements that includes punches, blocks, and kicks. The forms are flowing and powerful, like a dance. The moves mimic responses to an attack. Students do forms alone, without a partner or an opponent. Forms look somewhat like a gymnastics floor routine.

Students use forms to reach their next belt level. Tae kwon do teachers, called *sah bum nim* in Korean, judge their students' skills based on forms. The forms become more difficult to do as a student reaches higher belt levels.

WEAPONS

Weapons are usually an optional part of training in tae kwon do. The weapons used include swords, spears, nunchaku, and long and short staffs. The sword, also called Gum Do, is similar to a Japanese samurai sword. The nunchaku are two sticks connected by rope, leather, or chain. The long staff is similar to a pool cue. The short staff is like a baseball bat.

CHAPTER FOUR

COMPETITION

ompetition is a critical part of tae kwon do. It occurs at local, regional, and international levels, as well as at the Olympic Games.

The WTF and the ITF oversee many of the competitions. The WTF governs Olympic tae kwon do. The ITF runs the annual world championships. Several national and regional organizations host tournaments throughout the year. These include the U.S. Amateur Athletic Union, the World University Games, and the Asian Games. Events include board breaking, forms, self-defense, and sparring.

Girls competed in the 2003 Amateur Athletic Union Junior Olympic Games in Detroit, Michigan.

The speed of a flying kick helps a tae kwon do expert break a board.

BOARD BREAKING

In a breaking event, the goal is to break an object or a stack of objects. This shows speed, technique, and power. Boards vary in thickness. More skilled students break several boards stacked on top of one another. Competitors use different parts of their bodies to break the boards or the bricks. These include the head, the fists, the feet, and the elbows.

A team from Turkey demonstrated forms during a 2011 WTF event in Russia.

FORMS

A forms event has individual and team categories. Students demonstrate the forms in front of a panel of judges. Students are judged on accuracy, posture, confidence, and technical skill.

SELF-DEFENSE

Like forms, a self-defense event is a planned set of moves. One person faces several teammates who act as if they are attacking the competitor. The attacks and defense show the student's skill at defeating the attackers. Competitors are judged on how realistic the self-defense demonstration is. The variety of self-defense moves used is also important. Judges also look at the quality and difficulty of the techniques.

SPARRING

Of all the events, sparring is the most challenging and amazing. In this event, two fighters try to defeat one another with striking and kicking. Under the WTF's rules, sparring is full contact. This means the punches and kicks are done at full force. Two age divisions are set up. One is for 14 to 17 year olds. The second is for people 18 years old and older. These divisions are then broken down into weight divisions.

Matches have three rounds. The fighters score points based on how well they hit the scoring areas. Specific areas of the body are scoring areas. These include the head (for kicks only) and the torso (for strikes and kicks). The competitor with the most points at the end of the match wins the event. An overtime round is held if there is a tie. The judges determine the winner if neither competitor scores during the overtime.

Young tae kwon do students spar during training.

However, a big lead can also decide the winner. A fighter wins if he or she has a 12-point lead after the second or during the third round. The cleanest way to win is by knockdown. A knockdown happens when a competitor falls to the floor. A knockdown also happens if the competitor is staggering and unable to respond.

Sparring rules are similar for an ITF event. In the ITF, however, sparring is not full contact. Also, hand attacks are allowed to the head, and the scoring is slightly different.

OLYMPIC GAMES AND TAE KWON DO

The Olympic Games is the major event in tae kwon do for men and women. The four weight divisions are flyweight, featherweight, welterweight, and heavyweight.

South Korea has won the most Olympic gold medals in tae kwon do. China and the United States follow. In the 2008 Olympic tae kwon do event, South Korea ranked first. Mexico had the second spot. China was in third place. The United States finished fifth with one silver and two bronze medals.

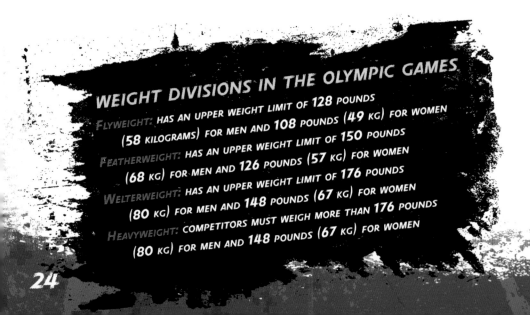

WEIGHT DIVISIONS IN THE OLYMPIC GAMES

FLYWEIGHT: HAS AN UPPER WEIGHT LIMIT OF 128 POUNDS (58 KILOGRAMS) FOR MEN AND 108 POUNDS (49 KG) FOR WOMEN

FEATHERWEIGHT: HAS AN UPPER WEIGHT LIMIT OF 150 POUNDS (68 KG) FOR MEN AND 126 POUNDS (57 KG) FOR WOMEN

WELTERWEIGHT: HAS AN UPPER WEIGHT LIMIT OF 176 POUNDS (80 KG) FOR MEN AND 148 POUNDS (67 KG) FOR WOMEN

HEAVYWEIGHT: COMPETITORS MUST WEIGH MORE THAN 176 POUNDS (80 KG) FOR MEN AND 148 POUNDS (67 KG) FOR WOMEN

Contestants competed in the 2010 European Police and Fire Games.

U.S. athletes Terrence Jennings and Paige McPherson are up-and-coming talents. They are Olympic hopefuls for the 2012 Olympic Games in London, England.

U.S. STARS

Top U.S. tae kwon do stars include Diana Lopez, Stephen Lambdin, Jennifer Daye, and Alex Ahlstrom. Lopez won an Olympic bronze medal in tae kwon do at the 2008 Olympic Games. Lambdin took the 2011 national collegiate championship in the men's heavyweight division. Daye won the 2011 national collegiate championship in the women's light division. Ahlstrom triumphed at the 2011 national collegiate championship in the men's light division.

Tae kwon do practitioner Anthony Pettis (right) punched Ben Henderson (left) during a World Extreme Cagefighting match in 2010.

MMA AND TAE KWON DO

Another arena for tae kwon do fighters is in mixed martial arts (MMA). Many fighters who go into MMA fight in the Ultimate Fighting Championship (UFC). This is the most popular MMA group in the United States. Some of the world's best MMA fighters have a tae kwon do base. They include Anthony Pettis, Bas Rutten, Anderson Silva, and Mauricio Rua. Pettis won the 2010 UFC World Extreme Cagefighting championship. Rutten is retired. But he stays involved with MMA by training fighters and commenting during matches. Silva was the 2011 UFC middleweight champion. Rua is considered among the top 10 MMA fighters in the world.

TRAINING THE FULL PERSON

Tae kwon do has many sides to it. It is used for self-defense. Events at the Olympic level are global and fierce. The martial art has become a key part of professional MMA fights. Students of tae kwon do learn self-discipline and gain self-confidence in many areas of life. Tae kwon do has millions of fans throughout the world.

TECHNIQUE HOW-TO

KNIFE HAND

A fighter begins with arms on the sides raised to the waist. The fighter punches one fist forward while the other hand is brought back to the ear. The hand that is brought back should be in the open knife hand striking position—hand out flat and straight with the thumb tucked against the side. Next, the fighter brings back the punching arm while at the same time extending the knife hand, striking the opponent with the outside edge of the hand.

SIDE KICK

A fighter begins with feet hip-width apart. Then one leg is lifted up to a 90-degree angle in front of the body. The leg is in what's called the kicking chamber. The fighter then rotates the hips and the bent leg so they are facing the side and then fires the foot straight out to the side.

A side kick

The kicking chamber for a front snap kick

FRONT SNAP KICK

A fighter begins with feet hip-width apart. Then one knee is raised into the kicking chamber. Next, the fighter fires the foot forward, kicking with the ball of the foot.

ROUNDHOUSE KICK

A fighter begins with feet hip-width apart with one leg back. The fighter bends the back leg and lifts the knee very high. Next, the fighter fires out the leg while spinning toward the opponent.

A roundhouse kick (left)

GLOSSARY

ACCURACY

performing moves that have no mistakes

MASTERS

persons who have achieved a high level of skill and who can teach others

PURITY

free of fault or guilt

STRIKE

any of the punches used in tae kwon do

TORSO

the midsection of the human body

UFC

the Ultimate Fighting Championship, which is an organization many MMA competitors fight in

FOR MORE INFORMATION

FURTHER READING

Gifford, Clive. *Martial Arts Legends.* New York: Crabtree Publishing, 2009.

Page, Jason. *Martial Arts, Boxing, and Other Combat Sports.* New York: Crabtree Publishing, 2008.

Park, Y. H. *Taekwondo for Kids.* Boston: Tuttle Publishing, 2005.

Wells, Garrison. *Karate: Japanese Empty-Hand Combat.* Minneapolis: Lerner Publications Company, 2012.

WEBSITES

International Taekwon-Do Federation
http://www.itftkd.org
The website of the International Taekwon-Do Federation includes information about events and news relating to the sport.

USA Taekwondo
http://usa-taekwondo.us
The official website of USA Taekwondo includes news, event information, and other resources about all levels of tae kwon do.

World Taekwondo Federation
http://www.wtf.org/
This website of the Olympic tae kwon do governing organization has information about the history and philosophy of tae kwon do, as well as photos, videos, and a hall of fame.

INDEX

ABOUT THE AUTHOR

Garrison Wells is a third-degree black belt in Nihon jujitsu, first-degree black belt in judo, third-degree black belt in Goju-ryu karate, and first-degree black belt in kobudo. He is also an award-winning journalist and writer. Wells lives in Colorado.